Acknowledgments

For me the dream of portraying my ideas visually, and being able to present them to a wide public has come true. My special thanks go especially to Christine Kelch of Triangle, photographer Thomas Schultze, as well as Petra Hundacker and Christine Birnbaum of HEEL Publishing, who were convinced by my concept. In addition, I would like to thank Hubert Stumpf of Moguntia for the prepared spices and marinades. Thanks also to the Cologne Handelshof for their support.

I would also like to mention the late school director, Mr. Arnold Trippner, for his support in this enterprise.

triangle®
WWW.TRIANGLE-TOOLS.DE

CONTENTS

Garnish & Decorating
Made Easy

Georg Hartung

With photographs by Thomas Schultze

4880 Lower Valley Road Atglen, Pennsylvania 19310

Creative Ideas for Garnishing and Decorating, 978-0-7643-3645-4, $19.99

Table Decoration with Fruits and Vegetables, 978-0-7643-3510-5, $24.99

Food Presentation: Tips & Inspiration, 978-0-7643-3481-8, $24.99

Originally published as *Garnieren & Verzieren leicht gemacht* by HEEL Verlag GmbH.

Text: Georg Hartung
Photos: Thomas Schultze
Layout: Claudia Reinerkens, reinerkens kommunikations-Design
Translated from the German by Dr. Edward Force

This book was written according to our best knowledge. Neither the author nor the publisher is liable for undesired outcomes that arise from the preparation of the ingredients herein.

Library of Congress Control Number: 2011941699

Type set in Minion Pro
ISBN: 978-0-7643-3932-5
Printed in China

Schiffer Books are available at special discounts for bulk purchases for sales promotions or premiums. Special editions, including personalized covers, corporate imprints, and excerpts can be created in large quantities for special needs. For more information contact the publisher:

Published by Schiffer Publishing Ltd.
4880 Lower Valley Road
Atglen, PA 19310
Phone: (610) 593-1777; Fax: (610) 593-2002
E-mail: Info@schifferbooks.com

For the largest selection of fine reference books on this and related subjects, please visit our website at
www.schifferbooks.com
We are always looking for people to write books on new and related subjects. If you have an idea for a book, please contact us at the above address.

This book may be purchased from the publisher.
Include $5.00 for shipping.
Please try your bookstore first.
You may write for a free catalog.

In Europe, Schiffer books are distributed by
Bushwood Books
6 Marksbury Ave.
Kew Gardens
Surrey TW9 4JF England
Phone: 44 (0) 20 8392 8585; Fax: 44 (0) 20 8392 9876
E-mail: info@bushwoodbooks.co.uk
Website: www.bushwoodbooks.co.uk

Foreword

The idea for this book has been in my mind for a long time. It originated in the course of my long years of activity as a cook, a butcher, and a teacher at a trade school for practical instruction for cooks, butchers, and butcher-shop employees. I noticed that many of my students lacked not only the courage but also the ideas to plate their prepared test dishes in a scene with suitable decorations. Everyone knows the saying, "The eyes eat too,"—but how does the eye attain the taste?

I would like to inspire you, dear readers, to try out decorations and trimmings that are quick and easy to prepare, and thus to surprise your guests or clients. I have deliberately not limited myself to decorating and trimming fruits and vegetables, but also show possible ways for you to present your little works of art when preparing meals. When you have become comfortable using the simple carving techniques, then any food product can serve as inspiration to let your imagination run wild. Just take the time and dedicate yourself with care to the creative, relaxing work of decorating and trimming, and thus surprise your family and friends.

I wish you a lot of pleasure in this endeavor!

Georg Hartung

Tips for Successful Garnishing and Decorating

Creative, diversified decorations made of fruits or vegetables are often the "dot on the i" of a culinary arrangement—they make the ultimate eye candy on a tastily prepared plate. It is important when shopping to be sure that you acquire faultless, fresh fruit, for this is an essential contribution to the success of the decorations and garnishes. In addition, you should always buy fresh fruits and vegetables in season when possible. Seasonal produce is not only tastier and has more nutrients, but is also more economical. And beyond that, you also do something for the environment when you, for example, do without strawberries for Christmas dinner but plan on them for a Pentecost brunch.

So that as many nutrients as possible remain in the fruits and vegetables, you should always cover them or store them where it is cool and dark. Special storage containers for foods, which are now on the market in many varieties, certainly are justified when you want to preserve something. You should never let vegetables lie in water for long, since the water-soluble vitamins would then be lost. Vegetables, as a rule, will naturally become tough, but with fresh ingredients and proper storage there is no need for soaking. Because of the nutrient loss, you should also just wash fruit briefly with water.

Light sliced fruits like bananas, apples, or pears will quickly turn brown. But if you drip a little lemon juice on the cut surfaces, you can avoid this.

When you prepare decorations, you should make absolutely sure that you use sharp knives and good tools, for this makes the work much easier. With low-priced tools you will hardly be able to create satisfactory results.

When you want to create appetizing and imaginative ham, sausage, or cheese platters, it is very important to consider the thickness of the slices. If they are cut too thin, they usually cannot be folded well or lack sufficient stability. Slices cut too thick, on the other hand, usually lose their shape. If you have a food slicer, your best bet is to buy product by the piece and slice them yourself, thus attaining the best results for your purposes. Note the slicing stability of the ingredient right afterward. Thus you don't need to test again next time.

It is best to have a butcher shop prepare meat slices for your purposes. This eliminates leftovers, and by going to a butcher, you are sure to get a bit of good advice.

The Hardware: The Knife and Its Helpers
KNIVES

The joy of making decorations out of food, and successful carving results, depend on your skill, the quality of the foods, and the usefulness of the tools. Good tools not only make the work easier, but let you create shapes and effects that cannot be made with a straight blade alone. So here is a small overview of the most important tools and what you can do with them.

Absolutely necessary for work with fruits and vegetables is a sharp and handy **vegetable and fruit paring knife.**

The fruit decorator cuts melons, papaya, squash, citrus, and many other fruits into decorative zigzag halves. To do so, the angled blades, sharpened on both edges, are pushed into the fruit all around and the two zigzag halves are separated.

With the help of **cutting tools** (V-knife, U-knife), flowers, rosettes, sculptures, and pictures can be filigreed from fruits and vegetables.

Melon ballers (from 3/4" to 1 1/8" diameter [20 to 30 mm]) are used to make balls of fruit, vegetable, or butter. Their upper edge should be sharpened.

The **fruit spoon** is sharpened and, because of its shape, very suitable for hollowing out melons, squash, eggplant, and other fruits and vegetables with pulp.

Vertical or other **peelers** are a must in the kitchen. No fruit can have its rind removed faster and more efficiently than with a peeler.

Potato spirals, large and small, similar to corkscrews, are twisted into potatoes, carrots, beets, radishes, or other hard vegetables. The results are cheery spirals, some 1/2" or 1" wide, which can be eaten raw, cooked, or fried.

With the sharp bar of a **notch knife,** patterns and ornaments can be carved into the surfaces or skins of fruits and vegetables. It is one of the favored tools in the art of carving vegetables.

The **chisel knife** is used to cut angles out of fruits and vegetables of varying hardness.

As with a pencil sharpener, radishes, carrots, beets, pears, or kohlrabi can be cut with a **spiral cutter** to brighten up a plate of raw vegetables, making it a colorfully decorated platter.

The **radish cutter** produces endless, evenly thick garlands of firm, long vegetables such as radishes, beets, zucchini, or turnips. It is used traditionally in Bavaria, where radishes are served lightly salted as a raw vegetable with white sausage and sweet mustard.

With the **wave cutter**, discs, pins, or cubes can be created with zigzag effects. Carrots, cucumbers, radishes, and kohlrabi are suitable, as are apples, melons, and papaya.

With the **julienne cutter**, carrots, zucchini, radishes, beets, and other vegetables can be cut into fine, even strips to make vegetable spaghetti, decorative cords, or matchstick-sized ingredients for soups.

The **fine plane** cuts slices of cucumbers, onions, root vegetables, truffles, and other mushrooms quickly and without trouble. A cutting blade, infinitely adjustable, allows very thin to thick slices. End pieces can also be worked without a problem.

The **butter roller** produces butter curls for decorative single portions on a buffet, a plate rim, or with meat.

To cut hard cheeses such as Gouda, cheddar, or Swiss into equally thick slices, the **wire cheese cutter** is the perfect instrument. It cuts the cheese into two different thicknesses. The wire can be tightened, and can always be replaced if it breaks.

Soft cheeses like Brie or Camembert, goat cheese, or Gorgonzola can be sliced best with a special **cheese knife**. Large cutouts in the blade prevent the cheese from sticking to the blade or being crushed.

The **needle** works like a sewing needle. With its help, meat bags, roasts, or poultry can be sewn up.

The elliptical shape of the **skewers** prevents the meat from turning around the skewer and being cooked on one side only. The meat can be loosened and removed easily from its smooth surface.

Whoever gladly and frequently prepares platters with slices of sausage or cheese can use the **carving fork** for fast, flexible work. With the help of the curved tines, the slices can be grasped simply. Two extra-large tines allow the slices to be rolled and served accurately.

Fruits

Apple Fan

1. For apple fans you need a small paring knife.

2. Cut a small V-shape into the side of the apple and pull the small apple piece out somewhat.

3. Now cut a somewhat larger V-shape around the first V and pull the second apple piece forward somewhat.

4. Repeat this process two or three more times, depending on how big your apple fans are supposed to be.

5. This apple fan consists of four V-shaped pieces.

So that the fans do not turn brown, immediately drip some lemon juice on them. Vitamin C powder dissolved in water works just as well.

APPLE SWAN

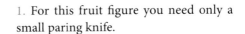

1. For this fruit figure you need only a small paring knife.

2. Halve the apple just past the core and cut the apple five times, as with the **APPLE FAN** (p. 14). Pull the apple slices apart.

3. Now cut a small apple fan with three slices on the left and right sides. Drip lemon juice on the separated slices so they do not turn brown.

4. Cut a thicker slice with no core off the other half of the apple, and cut a swan's neck out of it with the small paring knife. You may need to shape this some more on the outer edges (see photo).

5. Now stick a toothpick down into the large middle slices. With two peppercorns or dried cloves, make two eyes.

Finally, stick the swan's neck onto the toothpick, and your apple swan is finished.

DOUBLE STRAWBERRY FAN

1. The double strawberry fan is simple to make. You only need a small paring knife (3" [8 cm] blade).

2. Cut the leaves off a washed strawberry. Place the berry with the pointed side up. From above, cut slightly offset, halfway in.

3. Now place the knife perpendicular to the first cut and cut in (see photo). With this cut you have separated about one quarter of the strawberry.

4. Cut the quarter two more times from above and pull the slices apart like a fan. Turn the berry 180 degrees and do the same thing with the second quarter.

The result is double fans. You can also make single fans (see **APPLE FAN**, p. 14) of a strawberry.

ORANGE-KIWI STAR

1. The orange-kiwi star is easy to make with a V-knife or fruit decorator. Or you can also use a simple paring knife.

2. Cut a zigzag line in to the middle of the orange all the way around. Be sure to cut deeply enough into the fruit so you can later separate the two halves.

3. Do the same thing with the kiwi.

Separate the two halves from each other.

MELON BASKET

1. For the melon basket, use a fruit spoon, a fruit decorator, a small paring knife, and a cutting knife.

2. With the paring knife, cut into the melon twice from above to the middle. Make sure that in the middle of the melon a strip about 3/8" (1 cm) wide remains as a handle.

3. Cut into the melon all around with the fruit decorator, and then cut out the handle.

4. Lift the two pieces of melon off and remove the seeds with the fruit spoon.

5. Cut out the flesh on the handle with the V-knife, giving the underside of the handle a nice look.

Fill the melon basket with dragon fruit, melon, strawberry, and Peruvian cherries (Physalis peruviana), also called golden berries.

Place a strawberry star (see **KIWI STAR**, p. 20) on the handle with a toothpick as an added decoration.

MELON STAR

1. To make a melon star you need a fruit spoon and a fruit decorator.

2. Stick a fruit decorator evenly into a zigzag line around the middle of the washed melon. Alternatively, you can also use a small paring knife.

3. Make sure that you cut deeply enough. Then pull the zigzag-cut melon halves apart.

4. Remove the pulp with the help of a fruit spoon or deep spoon.

To give your melon star a flat surface to stand on, trim the round part of the melon.

A display of **FRUIT STARS**: melon, orange, kiwi, and strawberry.

Vegetables

KOHLRABI FLOWER

1. You need a small paring knife, a cutting knife, and a small melon baller to make this flower.

2. Peel the kohlrabi with the small knife and trim both ends. Stick the cutting knife (U-knife) into the middle of the vegetable, making a small circle about 3/4" (2 cm) deep.

3. Then carefully cut with the knife from the side of the kohlrabi to the circle in the center.

Lift the first cut piece out.

4. Use the U-knife to cut a ring of several petals around the center of the small flower. Then use the paring knife to cut from the side of the kohlrabi to below the petals just cut with the U-knife.

5. Repeat this process five to seven times. The size of the vegetable determines the number of layers.

6. For the last cut, cut down to the bottom of the kohlrabi, so as to make a neat rim.

For decoration, make a small ball of a red beet with the melon baller and place it on top of the kohlrabi flower.

You can also make this type of flower out of other firm vegetables, such as red beets, radishes, and turnips.

TOMATO ROSE

For the tomato rose you need a small paring knife (3" [8 cm] blade).

Cut most of one end of the tomato, so that a kind of raised lid results. Then peel the tomato in one piece, circling the fruit. Roll the tomato strip up from the end and put it on the lid.

SIMPLE ZUCCHINI-CARROT FLOWER

1. For this vegetable flower you need a vertical or other peeler (for the carrot) and a melon baller.

2. Peel the carrot and cut the lower 3/4" (2 cm) at an angle from four sides almost to the middle. Then carefully break the carrot flower off. Do the same with the zucchini, but do not peel it.

3. With a melon baller, cut a ball out of a radish and fasten it to the middle of the zucchini flower with a toothpick. Its red skin should be upward for color contrast. Do the same with the carrot flower, but make a ball of the white radish.

Small bouquet of zucchini and carrot flowers.

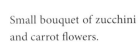

GRAPES of CUCUMBER

Grapes of Cucumber

For these grapes you need a notch knife, a paring knife, and a melon baller.

1. Cut the upper third of the cucumber off at a sharp angle.

2. With the knife, cut out two leaves and make small notches along the edges. Cut a stem out of the excess.

With the notch knife, cut small grooves in the upper sides of the leaves.

3. From the rest of the cucumber, use the melon baller to form the grapes. Depending on the size of the bunch of grapes that you want to make, you may need two or three cucumbers.

Arrange the balls in the shape of a bunch of grapes
and attach the stem and leaves above it.

FLOWER BOUQUET

For this bouquet you need a half-round cutter, two melon ballers of different sizes (2/5" and 7/8" [10 and 22 mm]), a small paring knife, and a leaf cutter mold (or a small paring knife, see **GRAPES OF CUCUMBER**, p. 34).

1. Cut a piece about 8" (20 cm) long from a radish and peel it. Cut a flat surface on one side so it lies stable.

In the middle of the piece, attach a cutout kohlrabi flower with a toothpick. Fasten a small ball of carrot in the middle of the flower as decoration.

2. Around the **KOHLRABI FLOWER** (see p. 30), attach three **TOMATO ROSES** (see p. 32) with toothpicks.

3. Under each of the tomato roses, attach a **ZUCCHINI FLOWER** and a **CARROT FLOWER** (see p. 33).

Keep the color contrast here.

With a leaf cutter mold, make five leaves from a zucchini or a cucumber. You can also make the leaves yourself (see p. 34).

Attach the leaves with toothpicks to create a small bouquet, with which you can surely delight your guests.

VEGETABLE STRIPS

2. Wash the zucchini and draw the julienne cutter along the length of the vegetable. Then you can brown the strips briefly and season with salt and pepper. Vegetable nests are suitable for poached eggs or fish dishes.

1. Vegetable strips are easy to make with a julienne cutter. Eggplant, zucchini, carrots, and other firm vegetables are suitable.

As a decoration, you can also set a **TOMATO ROSE** (see p. 32) on the vegetable nest.

CARROT FLOWER

1. The carrot flower is made with a vertical or other peeler, a small paring knife (3" [8 cm] blade) and a chisel knife.

2. Make five grooves along the length of the carrot with the chisel knife.

3. Then cut the carrot into thin slices.

Place alternating chiseled carrot and cucumber slices in a circle. Then set a **RADISH ROSE** (see p. 46) in the middle.

CARROT-RADISH SPIRALS

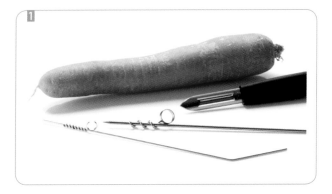

1. The tools you need for this job are a peeler and a potato spiral (large and/or small).

2. Peel the washed carrot (or the white radish) and cut off both ends. Now turn the potato spiral carefully in the middle of the carrot.

3. As you turn the spiral, be sure that the tool is completely straight in the vegetable. Turn the spiral completely around the vegetable.

4. Then turn the big spiral back again carefully. Attach the spiral with the point of a paring knife and turn the housing clockwise. You can simply pull the small spirals out of the housing.

Then strip the spirals off the potato spiral and decorate the pieces as you wish.

LEEK FLOWER

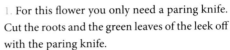

1. For this flower you only need a paring knife. Cut the roots and the green leaves of the leek off with the paring knife.

2. Quarter the leek, though not all the way to the end. The individual leaves should still hold together at the end.

3. Cut the leek ends off diagonally and wash the vegetable.

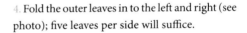
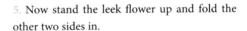

4. Fold the outer leaves in to the left and right (see photo); five leaves per side will suffice.

5. Now stand the leek flower up and fold the other two sides in.

Cut the longer leaves off in the middle, so that the upper folded-in leaves stand somewhat higher.

For decoration, you can place a **RADISH STAR** (p. 20) in the middle and put a small zucchini ball on top.

RADISH SHAPES

For these radish figures you need a paring knife.

SIMPLE RADISH FLOWER

Cut off the greens and root of the radish. Then cut it deeply four or five times, just off the center, and put it in cold water. In the water the radish will spread out and unfold to form a flower.

THE RADISH CONE

Trim the greens and the small root off the radish. Cut into the radish from three sides, from top to bottom, with the paring knife. Let the radish soak in water for about 20 minutes, so that the cuts become clearer.

TIP:
The radish cone is especially suitable for decorating cheese, sausage, or ham platters.

THE RADISH MOUSE

Choose a radish with some greens and root. Cut it lenthwise so that the greens (for the nose) and the root (for the tail) remain on one half. From the other half, cut out the right and left ears with the paring knife.

Slit the radish in its front third and stick the ears into the cuts (with the white side forward). The root remains as the tail. In front of the ears, make two small holes for the eyes with a toothpick. You can use cloves or black peppercorns. Push the eyes in firmly.

RADISH ROSE

Radish Rose

1. For the radish rose, it is best to use a fine plane. You can also use a slicing machine or a sharp knife.

2. Plane thin slices off a washed and peeled radish.

3. Roll a radish slice into a snail shape and hold it firmly by its lower end. Surround the stem with three white petals, still holding the lower end in one hand. Then surround the rose blossom with five more petals. Use toothpicks to hold them in place when you can no longer hold them in one hand.

This radish rose was colored with red beet juice.

A small bouquet with tomato roses. This decoration goes well on sausage or ham platters.

RED BEET SPIRALS

Red Beet Spirals

1. For the red beet spiral you need a radish cutter, a peeler, and a large knife.

2. Peel the beet and cut the sides in a hexagonal form. Cut the two ends off flat. Stick the guide rod of the radish cutter in the middle and twist the threading into the beet.

3. By cutting circularly into the beet with the blade, you produce a spiral as long as you want.

Pull the guide rod out of the vegetable and arrange your spiral in a circle on a plate or platter. For contrast, put some **RADISH ROSES** (see p. 46) in the middle of the spiral. Red beet or radish spirals can be used for garnishing small platters and in preparing raw-food platters.

ASIAN ZUCCHINI FAN

1. For this fan, which is very easy to make, you need a small paring knife.

2. Wash the zucchini and cut off the stem. Now separate a section 3 1/8" to 3.5" (8 to 9 cm) long and halve it.

Cut into the halved zucchini piece two to twelve times in a fan shape. Be sure not to cut through the vegetable; leave the individual strips attached at one end.

3. Blanch the cut zucchini piece briefly. Chill it briefly and alternately bend every other strip to the left or right.

Along with a **TOMATO ROSE** (see p. 32), this decoration looks very good with pasta dishes.

ZUCCHINI SPIRALS

Zucchini Spirals

1. For this spiral you need a notch knife or chisel knife, a paring knife, and a spiral cutter.

2. Cut off the stem of a washed zucchini and make about eight lengthwise cuts with a notch or chisel cutter.

3. Turn the zucchini in the spiral cutter like a pencil in a sharpener.

4. Turn the zucchini until a garland is formed.

Add small **CARROT FLOWERS** (see p. 39), which you can also make with the spiral cutter. The two combine to make a colorful decoration.

Meat

PINEAPPLE SKEWER
MEAT POCKETS
MEAT PURSE
WAVED SKEWER

PINEAPPLE SKEWER

Pineapple Skewer

From left to right:
For the pineapple skewer you need two skewers, a sharp knife, strips of turkey breast (or pork fillet), and several slices of pineapple.

Have long turkey strips cut for you in a butcher shop. They should be about 1" (2.5 cm) thick and 6" (15 cm) long. Cut the strips into five cubes of equal size. Marinate them in a marinade (here curry marinade) or season them with salt and pepper. Cut a pineapple into chunks of similar size and put them on a skewer, alternating with the meat cubes.

TIP:
If you do not plan on cooking and serving the skewers right away, use pineapple from a can, since fresh pineapple contains a strong acid that affects the taste.

PREPARATION:

Brown the marinated skewer in a pan on all sides at about 325°F (170°C). Put it on a baking sheet and bake it in the oven for about ten minutes at about 320°F (160°C).

Meanwhile baste the frying liquid from the pan with 3 1/3 Tablespoons (50 ml) of pineapple juice. Then add 1 1/3 Tablespoons (8 grams) of flour to it and stir it all together thoroughly. Next add 7/8 cup (200 ml) of sweet cream and let the sauce cook down until it is creamy.

Season the sauce with curry powder, salt, and pepper, and serve it with the pineapple skewers. Buttered rice goes well with it.

MEAT POCKETS

Meat Pockets

1. Cut a butterfly steak weighing 1/3 lb (~150 to 160 grams) from a pork loin. You can also use veal or turkey.

2. Fill the meat pockets with fruit (pineapple, dragon fruit, kiwi), fold it and keep it shut with two toothpicks to keep the filling in the pockets.

3. Season the meat pocket with salt and pepper, then dredge it first in flour, then in beaten egg, and finally in coconut flakes.

PREPARATION:

Fry the meat pockets on all sides in a pan at medium heat for 4 to 5 minutes. Be very sure of the temperature, since the coconut coating will burn at higher temperatures, while the meat pockets will not be done yet.

If you use a firm filling, such as ground meat, the cooking time will be longer.

You can serve a curry sauce (see **PINEAPPLE SKEWER**, p. 54) with this meat specialty.

MEAT PURSE

Meat Purse

1. Have your butcher cut butterfly steaks (pork, veal, or turkey) weighing 1/3 lb (150 to 160 grams) each. Pound the steaks fairly flat soon after purchasing.

2. To make the meat bags you need a culinary needle and some firm kitchen twine. Thread a piece of twine (some 15 3/4" to 19 1/3" [40 to 50 cm]) in the eye of the needle.

3. With the needle, make stitches about 3/8" (1 cm) long around the steak. Be sure that you have enough thread to pull the bag together after filling it. Various fruits can be used as filling. Only use acidic fruits, like fresh kiwi, if you are preparing and serving the meat bags right away (see **PINEAPPLE SKEWER,** p. 54).

When you have filled the bags, pull the two ends of the thread together and knot them. Season the meat with some salt, pepper, and garlic powder, or with a mild curry mixture.

PREPARATION:

Brown the meat bags briefly on all sides in a pan. Put them on a baking sheet and bake them in the oven at 320°F (160°C) for 15 to 20 minutes. The baking time also depends on the filling. Dense fillings like ground meat need more time to cook through. While the bags are baking in the oven, baste the liquid in the pan with some pineapple juice 3 1/3 Tablespoons (50 ml). Then add about 1 1/3 Tablespoons (8 grams) of flour and 7/8 cup (200 ml) of sweet cream. Let the sauce cook down until it is creamy.

If necessary, season the sauce with curry powder, salt, and pepper, and serve it with the baked meat purse.

Buttered rice goes well with them.

WAVED SKEWER

Waved Skewer

From left to right:

For the waved skewer you need a skewer, a sharp knife, and pieces of pork loin.

Have a butcher cut a slab of pork loin or turkey breast about 3/8" (1 cm) thick and 8" (20 cm) long. The slab should be about 4 3/4" (12 cm) wide.

Cut the slab of meat into thirds and marinated the strips (here in a paprika marinade), or season them with salt and pepper.

Bend the meat strips into a waved shape and put them on the meat skewer. The number of strips depends on the length of the skewer. In this picture three meat strips were used for the skewer.

PREPARATION:

Brown the waved skewer on each side in a pan for a minute. Then put them on a baking sheet and bake them in the oven at 320°F (160°C) for 5 to 7 minutes.

Sauté about 1 Tablespoon (10 grams) of onion cubes in the pan with some butter. Add 1/2 cup (30 grams) of fresh mushroom slices and brown them for about one minute.

Baste the mushrooms with 2 Tablespoons (30 ml) of white wine. Dust the wine with about 1 1/3 Tablespoons (8 grams) of flour, add 7/8 cup (200 ml) of sweet cream, and cook the sauce down until it is creamy. Season the sauce with salt, pepper, garlic, and some tarragon, and serve it with the meat skewer.

Serve two skewers per portion. Noodles, croquettes, or rice will go well with them.

SHRIMP SKEWER
CHICKEN SKEWER
LIVER MOUSSE ON CRACKERS
CREAM CHEESE ON CUCUMBER
SWEET TEMPTATION

Finger Food

SHRIMP SKEWER

Shrimp Skewer

SUGGESTION: ·
Serve the finished
skewers stuck
into half a lemon.
A sweet and sour
sauce is very
good for dipping.

For this finger food you need jumbo shrimp, salt, pepper, a lemon, a Peruvian cherry (Physalis peruviana), and a small skewer. For breading you will use flour, egg, and coconut flakes.

First, halve a lemon lengthwise (see picture). Season the jumbo shrimp with salt, pepper, and lemon juice.

Dredge them in flour, then in beaten egg, and finally in coconut flakes.

Fry the shrimp in a pan with butter and some oil at medium heat.

Stick a jumbo shrimp on the skewer, then add a Peruvian cherry with husk (as pictured).

CHICKEN SKEWER

Chicken Skewer

For a chicken skewer you need three small cubes of chicken breast, a small skewer, salt, pepper, or a marinade for seasoning.

Stick the three chicken cubes on the skewer and season them with salt and pepper, or with a marinade. Brown the skewer on both sides at medium heat in a pan with some butter and oil for one minute at most. Serve it on a salad of mango and orange strips and pomegranate seeds.

SERVING TIP:
Serve the skewers with the fruit salad in small edible pastry cups with some sweet and sour sauce.

LIVER MOUSSE ON CRACKERS

Liver Mousse on Crackers

You need a paring knife and a piping bag with a star nozzle for this hors d'oeuvre. You also need some delicatessen liverwurst (~1 oz. [25 g]), a radish, watercress, and a cracker per serving.

Whip some 2/3 lb (300 grams) of liverwurst airily with a hand mixer. Put the liverwurst into a piping bag with a star nozzle and pipe about 1 oz (25 grams) on a cracker.

Always hold the piping bag vertically and pipe a snail shape. Then cut deeply into a radish in zigzag form (see **KIWI STAR,** p. 20) and put the radish star on the liver mousse. For color contrast, put some cress behind the star.

CREAM CHEESE ON CUCUMBER

Cream Cheese on Cucumber

For this finger food you need a slice of cucumber 3/4" (2 cm) thick, cream cheese in a piping bag with star nozzle, a Peruvian cherry, a grape, and some watercress, plus a paring knife and a melon baller.

Hollow out the cucumber slice somewhat with the melon baller, pipe 1 oz (25 grams) of cream cheese into the recess in a snail shape, and garnish with a piece of Peruvian cherry and a slice of grape. Add watercress for color contrast. If you would like to season this hors d'ouevre a bit more strongly, then simply cut very small cubes of chili pepper and mix them with the cream cheese.

SWEET TEMPTATION

You need a disc of biscuit dough, chocolate mousse, a Peruvian cherry, a grape, a strawberry, and mint leaves.

If you don't find a biscuit disc, you can also buy a biscuit bottom and cut it out with a ring cutter.

Prepare a chocolate mousse and put it in a piping bag with a plain nozzle. Squeeze the mousse onto the biscuit disc in the shape of waves.

Then cut the fruits into slices and set them on the biscuit disc (see picture of strawberry, grape, and Peruvian cherry). For decoration, lay mint leaves in the middle.

Platters and Canapés

CHEESE PLATTER

Cheese Platter

To prepare the cheese platter, choose cheese types that vary in form, color, and taste. In the example shown here we use Tilsit, Gouda, Babybel, some hard mold cheese, Mozzarella, and Langres (a French soft cheese) garnished with dragon fruit, grapes, orange, and kiwi.

1. To be able to cut cheese slices equally and without sticking, a wire cheese cutter (for hard cheese) and a cheese knife (for soft cheese) is helpful.

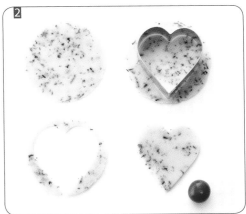

2. Cookie cutters can be used to shape cheese (see photo); depending on the type, one can use the remaining cheese, for example, in a cheese salad or for baking.

3. Cut the Tilsit, Gouda, or other slicing cheese in broad strips and lay them in two rows. You can now place the small round fresh cheeses in the middle.

4. Now lay wedges of mold cheese left and right of the rows of sliced cheese and arrange four Babybels on them, having removed half the cheese's wax covering.

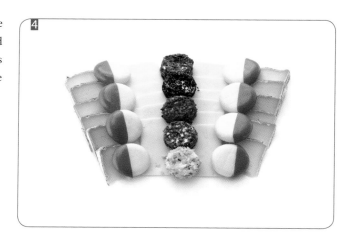

5. Now lay the cutout cheese hearts to the left and right. For this, use a cheese without holes that is cut somewhat thicker. As shown here, it is best to alternate two different kinds of cheese in this row. Thus you make a nice contrast, and the cutout cheese makes a good impression.

6. For the right arch, sliced mold cheese was used here. On the left side, a butter cheese with paprika was formed in an arch.

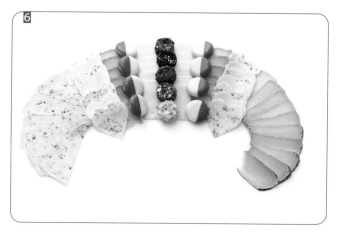

7. The lower arch was laid out with a sliced Gouda.

8. Now fill in the last two gaps with rows of alternating Mozzarella and tomato slices.

9. In the right corner is Langers, a soft cheese.

Decorate the cheese platter with two kiwi and one orange star, plus red and white grapes (see **ORANGE** and **KIWI STARS,** p. 20).

A cheese platter should consist of at least five or six kinds of cheese. Nobody likes every kind of cheese.

Also, be careful choosing the types, as they should harmonize with each other.

Techniques

HAM ROLLS

From left to right: Lay a ham slice on your work surface and roll it evenly with a carving fork.

Inside it you can put a stalk of asparagus, but be careful to let the asparagus end show.

HAM CONES

From left to right: Cut a slice of ham to the center and wrap the right side of the cut under the left to form a cone.

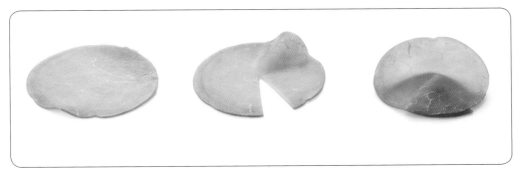

FOLDED SLICE

From left to right: Simply fold a ham or cold-cut slice one-third under.

SKIRT

From left to right: Fold a slice of prosciutto over itself four times (see photo). Press the lower end together, so that the ham slice retains its shape.

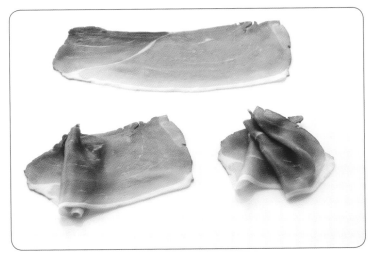

HAM PLATTER

1. Place four ham rolls with asparagus on a round platter.

2. Now put three more rolls on the lower four. Be sure that the rolls are always a bit staggered. Now put two more on them, and finish with one last ham roll on top.

3. Repeat this process on the opposite side. Be sure that the rolls are placed exactly and in the right order.

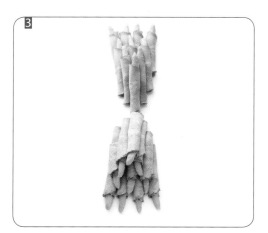

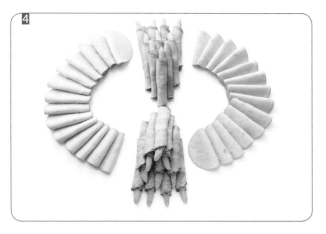

4. Now put folded slices (of turkey breast) in semicircles to the right and left, but leave spaces between the ham rolls and the turkey breast.

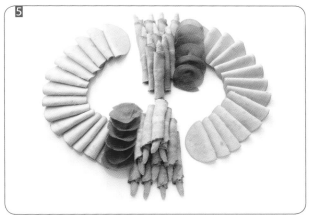

5. Put six salmon slices formed as cones to the right, beside the ham and asparagus rolls.

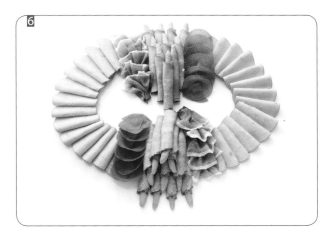

6. Fold strips of prosciutto into skirts (see **TECHNIQUES,** p. 77) and place five to the left of the ham and asparagus rolls.

7. Now fill the left gap with some turkey breast and/or cooked ham.

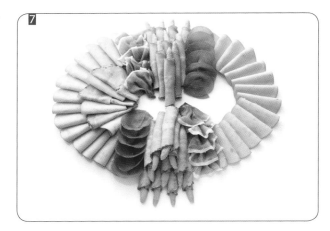

8. Repeat on the other side.

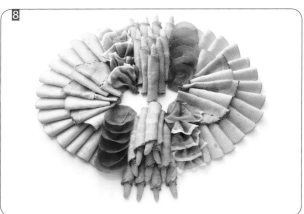

9. Now put two roses made of red beets and three radish roses in the middle. Be sure that the center of the platter is well covered.

To finish, garnish the plate with cucumber or zucchini leaves (see **GRAPES,** p. 34). You can also use a leaf cutter to make the leaves.

CANAPÉS

Canapés

Canapés are usually buttered toast (shown here) or white bread pieces without crust, topped with meat, sausage, cheese, eggs, or fish. Make sure the decorations harmonize with the toppings.

To cut the bread, it is best to use a round cutter about 2 1/3" (6 cm) in diameter, with appropriately smaller cutters for the cheese and a star shape for the paprika.

From top left to right:
Spread the cutout bread with butter (or mayonnaise). Cover with a slice of salami the size of the bread.

Cut out two somewhat smaller salami slices, wrap into cones (see **TECHNIQUES,** p. 77), and place on the canapé. Decorate each cone with a slice of olive stuffed with pimento and some watercress, and lay a halved baby corn on one side of the cone.

From top left to right:
Spread the bread with butter and cover with a slice of cheese (such as Gouda) cut out to the same size. Cut a slightly smaller disc of light dill cheese and add it with an even smaller disc of Gouda on top. The different shades of cheese provide a nice contrast. Fill a piping bag with a star nozzle with cream cheese and squeeze a small snail onto the middle. Garnish with a Peruvian cherry star and half of a red grape slice.

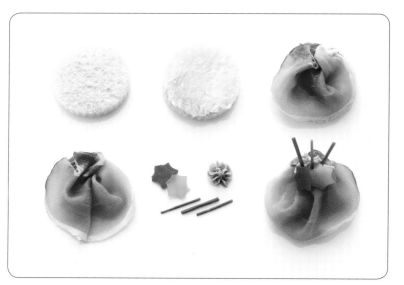

From top left to right:
Prepare the bread as for the cheese canapé, but use prosciutto (**SKIRT TECHNIQUE,** p. 77).

The garnish for this canapé consists of a small rosette of liver mousse (see **LIVER MOUSSE,** p. 64), two cutout pepper stars (yellow and red), and three small sprigs of chive.

From top left to right:
Spread the bread with mayonnaise and cover with a cutout disc of turkey breast of the same size. Cut a second turkey disc the same size, fold it to the middle from left and right, and place it on the middle of the canapé. At the end of the folded slice pipe on a rosette of cream cheese and decorate with a tomato rose made from a cocktail tomato (see **TOMATO ROSE,** p. 32), two yellow pepper strips, and three slices of a halved pickle.

Always make the rows of canapés with alternating light and dark toppings. In addition, every type of canapé should be garnished identically, to create a nice overall picture.

Decorations

BUTTER DECORATIONS
COCOA DECORATIONS

BUTTER DECORATIONS

Butter Decorations

WAVED BUTTER STICK

For this butter decoration you need a waved or similar cutter.

Be sure that the butter is cold. Dip the cutter briefly into hot water and then cut off a slice of the butter, about 1/8" (5 mm) thick. Separate the butter slice diagonally with the cutter to create two long, thin triangles.

This butter shape can be served with cold appetizers.

BUTTER SNAIL

For this decoration you need a butter roller.

Set the cold butter up on its longer side and draw the butter roller over it, creating small snails.

This form of butter is suitable for cold appetizers or buffets.

GRAPES OF BUTTER

The tools you need to make butter grapes are a small paring knife (3 1/8" [8 cm] blade) and a melon baller.

Be sure that the butter is very cold, otherwise it will not come out of the ball cutter smoothly. First, cut off two slices of butter with the paring knife, and cut two leaves and a stem (see **GRAPES of CUCUMBER**, p. 36). Then dip the melon baller in hot water and make balls of the remaining butter. Depending on the size of the grapes, you will need two or three 1/2-lb (250-gram) packages of butter.

TIP:
After scooping each ball, dip the baller in hot water to make smooth, evenly shaped balls.

Now place the butter balls in the form of a bunch of grapes. Put the two leaves and the stem above the grapes. This butter decoration is especially suitable for cold buffets or platters.

COCOA DECORATIONS

Cocoa Decorations

1. For cocoa decorations you need cocoa powder, a fine-mesh sieve, a spoon, and a kitchen fork.

2. Put some cocoa powder in the fine sieve and hold the fork and spoon on one edge of the plate. Cover the utensils with the cocoa.

Now lift the utensils carefully from the plate, and the decoration is finished.

Panna Cotta with cinnamon cherries makes a great dessert. Decorate with a **KIWI** and a **STRAWBERRY STAR** (see p. 20) as fruit garnish, as well as three small **APPLE FANS** (see p. 14). When you make up a dessert plate with three elements, a harmonious picture results.

PREPARING THE PANNA COTTA

2 cups (1/2 liter) cream
1/4 cup (40 grams) sugar
2/3 Tablespoon (9 grams) gelatin
1 Tablespoon (12 grams) vanilla sugar
1 vanilla pod

Soften the gelatin with some cream and melt it carefully over low heat. Warm the liquid cream, sugar, and vanilla. Mix the melted gelatin into the cream.

Pour the mixture into round forms or coffee cups, and let them cool in the refrigerator.

Warm the containers of Panna Cotta briefly in hot water, tip them onto a dessert plate, and garnish them.

Table Decoration: with Fruits and Vegetables. Angkana and Alex Neumayer. Learn to create remarkable decorations for the table and garnishes for glasses and plates. Many tips, 440 color photos, and practical, step-by-step directions guide you through works of art that are easy to produce. Carve a flower, shape a fish, a bell, the sun, and the moon. You will be adding light touches to your meals from here forward.
Size: 8 1/2" x 11" • 440 color photos • 128 pp.
ISBN: 978-0-7643-3510-5 • hard cover • $24.99

Creative Ideas for Garnishing & Decorating. Elisabeth Bangert. Step up your plating and decorating techniques with this ideal cookbook for those who regularly entertain. A wide spectrum of ingredients and products, including fruits and vegetables, dairy, meat, chocolate, and marzipan demonstrate just how creative you can be. More than 330 images capture step-by-step procedures. Includes holiday-specific ideas.
Size: 8 1/2" x 11" • 339 color photos • 80 pp.
ISBN: 978-0-7643-3645-4 • hard cover • $19.99

Schiffer books may be ordered from your local bookstore, or they may be ordered directly from the publisher by writing to:
Schiffer Publishing, Ltd.
4880 Lower Valley Rd.
Atglen, PA 19310
(610) 593-1777; Fax (610) 593-2002
E-mail: Info@schifferbooks.com

Please visit our web site catalog at www.schifferbooks.com or write for a free catalog. Please include $5.00 for shipping and handling for the first two books and $2.00 for each additional book. Full-price orders over $150 are shipped free in the U.S.

Printed in the United States of America